wisdom for relationships

Rhonda Pritchard

PENGUIN BOOKS

PENGUIN BOOKS
Penguin Books (NZ) Ltd, cnr Airborne and Rosedale Roads, Albany, Auckland 1310, New Zealand
Penguin Books Ltd, 27 Wrights Lane, London W8 5TZ, England
Penguin USA, 375 Hudson Street, New York, NY 10014, United States
Penguin Books Australia Ltd, 487 Maroondah Highway, Ringwood, Australia 3134
Penguin Books Canada Ltd, 10 Alcorn Ave, Toronto, Ontario, Canada M4V 3B2

Penguin Books Ltd, Registered Offices: Harmondsworth, Middlesex, England

First published by Penguin Books (NZ) Ltd, 1997

3 5 7 9 10 8 6 4

Typeset by Alison Dench
Printed in Hong Kong by Condor Production

Introduction

When the larger version of *Love in the Real World* was published I was often asked to describe the main idea in a few words. My glib response was that if I could have conveyed a message about close relationships in a T-shirt slogan I wouldn't have written a book. There is nothing simple about human beings: what is said in a few words rarely tells the whole story.

It's fun to try though.

Most of the thoughts contained in this book are my own, but there are some that have been offered by friends, colleagues and mentors from my past. There are also some that I may have unknowingly 'adopted' from other sources. I am sorry I cannot acknowledge every contributor to the collection – all I can do is mention those I can identify. These are, from the inner circle, Pam Hyde, Gordon Hewitt, Annie McGregor, Mig Wright, Colin Boswell and Ros Broadmore; and from the outer circle, Bob Goulding, Frederick Perls and Hazel Ross. My daughter Gabrielle Pritchard and my partner Julian Parsons also played their parts.

Beginnings

Loneliness is not life-threatening

– at least not in small doses.

‘I just want to be happy.’

All the time?

For adults, love is not

necessary for survival . . .

. . . it just helps a lot.

Waiting for love at first sight,

or until someone meets eight

out of ten pre-selected criteria,

could be a lifetime occupation.

Faith, hope and love –

but the most useless of them all

is hope.

The courtship dance should be

a minuet – not a lambada.

Somebody wanting to be my lover

is not necessarily wanting

to be my partner.

Niceness is not necessarily a good quality in a prospective partner . . .

. . . they'll be tempted to please

whoever is in front of them.

When choosing a partner

it's wise to choose a peer.

Passion is ephemeral and

makes a relationship hot.

Compassion lasts longer and

keeps it warm . . .

. . . but physical attraction is

a good start.

If we can't talk contraception,

we're not close enough,

or old enough, to make love.

At the height of intimacy,

it's likely one of us will fear being

abandoned while the other

will fear being engulfed.

If you tell me you love me,

I'll hope it means you choose me.

If you tell me you adore me,

I'll worry what will happen

if I do something wrong.

If you say, 'You're my whole life,'

I don't feel comforted –

I feel suffocated.

‘Till death us do part’

means one of us will end up alive . . .

. . . and alone.

If we marry too soon

we're probably in love with

an idea.

Grown-ups make better partners.

It is not surprising

that people go to weddings

and don't know whether

to laugh . . .

. . . or to cry.

Marriage

is not just a bit of paper.

It turns a partner into a relative

– a member of the family.

I promise

- to be loyal to you
- to be open with you and respectful towards you
- to put you and our children ahead of others
- to care for you if you are sick or troubled
- to play my part in your family, and
- to stand beside you as you live your own life.

Feelings

Love is like any feeling.

It comes and goes . . .

. . . and comes and goes.

Let's start with the feelings

I do have, not the feelings

I think I ought to have.

Just because my teeth are showing,

it doesn't mean I'm smiling.

If I had to choose,

I'd sacrifice being told I am loved

for being treated well.

Being more emotionally expressive

does not make me

a superior human being.

Guilt warns us there is a gap between

our values and our actions.

Guilt makes me feel bad

for someone else.

Shame makes me feel bad for myself.

The green eye of jealousy?

It's more a deep red or purple.

It burns and surges and turns us ugly.

Jealousy is not sick.

It just makes us *feel* sick.

In every one of us there's a small child

yearning for love that's exclusive.

If this is offered, then withdrawn,

of course we'll protest.

Fear is a useful emotion.

It stops us doing stupid things.

Cold anger may burn more

than hot anger.

Happiness is not a state

to be reached.

Back to Basics

Love in the real world is not always

'ups and downs' –

it's more often a bit flat.

The good-enough relationship:

- commitment
- loyalty
- safety, freedom and a sense of equality
- goodwill, respect and tolerance
- time and togetherness.

Oh, the comfort of knowing

someone is making life decisions

that take me into account.

Commitment means I'll stay with you,

even on the days I don't love you.

The threat to leave is

a dangerous weapon

– it backfires.

What attracted us earlier

may well be the problem later.

If I'm married to my mirror image,

one of us is redundant.

A question.

What's the most sympathetic

interpretation that could be made

about your partner's most

irritating habit?

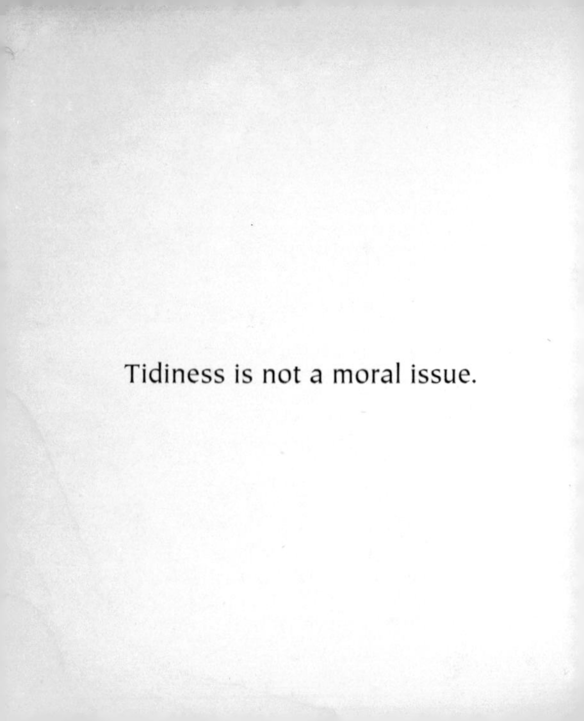
Tidiness is not a moral issue.

Familiarity breeds content.

A turning point: when we stop struggling and start accepting the differences between us.

Let's start with politeness.

We reward and punish each other

at about the same rate,

but using different methods.

Only a tiny proportion of people
are psychopaths.
Most of our transgressions are the
result of thoughtlessness, ignorance,
self-protection, avoidance, bad habits
or a need to discharge damage we feel
has been done to us.

Loss of respect is more of a risk to a relationship than loss of desire.

We cannot make love to a partner

who acts like a parent or a child.

That's incest.

I claim the freedom to

- be angry or upset
- spend time away
- have my own friends
- decline sexual approaches
- have and spend money.

Tolerance helps a relationship,

but some things are intolerable.

Drunkenness, drug abuse, aggression

or extreme possessiveness are

life-threatening . . .

. . . get help or go.

There's nothing wrong with

wanting power –

power to, not power over.

A bit of control has its place too.

Over some part of my *own* life.

A problem for one partner is

a problem for the couple.

Unconditional love is neither a right

nor a universal experience.

Only babies can mess the carpet

and still be loved.

Assumptions are the shaky

launching pad for many of our actions.

They project us into the

dangerous territory of believing we

know what is good for somebody else.

It's not my partner's job

to make my life interesting.

'How can I make my partner

- tidier?
- more expressive?
- more playful?
- more thoughtful?'

You can't – unless he or she wants to.

A relationship is always

a work in progress.

When we start using the term
'quality time', it usually means
life is too full and we may be
neglecting someone important.

You want to keep your relationship

exciting and passionate?

You might have to settle for intimacy.

Relationships thrive on

two kinds of intimacy –

face-to-face and side-by-side.

Intimacy of any kind does not flourish

in an atmosphere of obligation,

inequality or fear.

‘Working at’ a relationship

needn’t be a chore.

How about ‘playing in’ a relationship?

A question.

What's one thing you could

do today to give your partner

a pleasant surprise?

Don’t confuse needs with rights.

If the urge for the excitement

of an affair is irresistible,

hang-gliding and bungy jumping

are great alternatives.

I am sexually loyal not only because

my partner doesn't deserve

to be hurt or deceived.

Being faithful is psychologically and

morally more peaceful for *me*.

I confuse myself less and

like myself more.

The need for sex is not the same

as the need for water and food.

We can survive without it . . .

. . . just.

Treating sex as currency,

to be requested, given or withheld,

defeats its best purpose.

Most sexual problems

are problems of desire.

A question.

What did you do together when

you first met that you don't do now?

If there is tension about money and
power there's a practical solution.
Divide it into three parts: our money,
your money and my money.

Dividing human beings into

men and women

is a crude way to classify them.

There's more variation within the

genders than between the genders.

Forget Mars and Venus.

Men and women live on Earth.

While our children may be

our major purpose, they are also

our greatest stress.

Our own children have needs.

Other people's children

make demands.

Don't ask your partner to choose

between you and their children.

If they're worth their salt

they'll choose their children.

Children need love, limits and liberty.

Adults too.

Communication

A secret is something we tell
one person at a time.

Not every problem in a relationship is

a result of poor communication.

'I don't love you' is as clear

a piece of communication

as you can get.

Not all feelings need to be expressed.

Honesty is a virtue. So is tact.

We cannot avoid communicating.
There is nothing so eloquent as
a tense voice, a stony silence, a long
sigh, a pointed finger and a thump on
the chair arm.

‘Do you want to go out?’

‘Oh I dunno. Do you want to?’

For God’s sake, say what you want.

Too much distance and we'll fight our way back to closeness.

Complaining about how distant we

are will not bring us closer.

Don’t burn up on re-entry.

'I've said I'm sorry.

What more do you want?'

Say it again . . .

. . . and again.

There's no point in asking,

'How was your day?'

unless we listen to the answer.

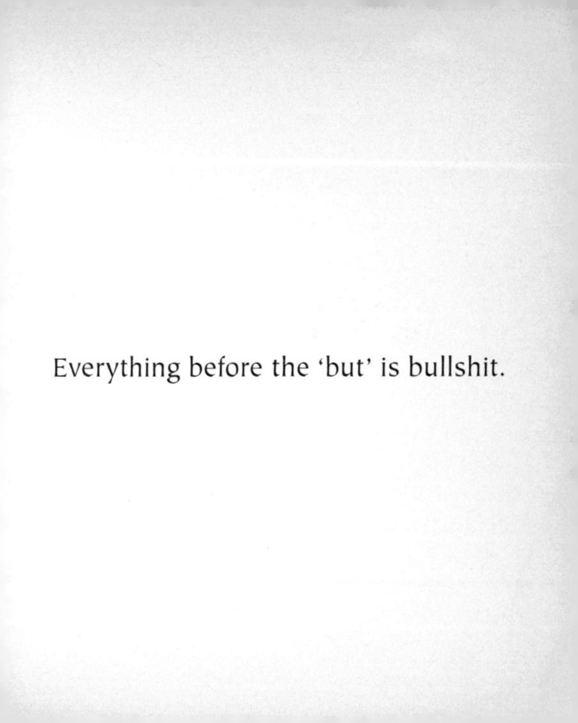
Everything before the ‘but’ is bullshit.

Criticising someone else is often

a way of congratulating myself.

Criticism cuts deeper than praise,

and the effects last longer.

‘Don’t take this personally.’

‘So, are you not talking about me?’

Many of us grow up in families that believe too much praise is bad for us, so we offer the same diet to others – dry bread and cheese.

Appreciations, regular and specific,

put money in the bank.

Conflict

A little bit of conflict keeps

a relationship alive.

A healthy relationship thrives when

it's safe to be angry –

but not too often and not too much.

The one who refuses to talk is
contributing to the fight just as much
as the one who won't stop talking.

Most fights start with an issue.

They end with a fight about

how we fight.

Don't compromise unless you can

be sure you will not keep score.

Being right or winning the argument

may put us out in front or up on top,

but rarely alongside.

Many rows are variations on a theme:

'Why can't you be more like me!'

Under stress we regress.

Sometimes we need to choose

between peace and justice.

Endings

If you make one more ultimatum,

I'm leaving.

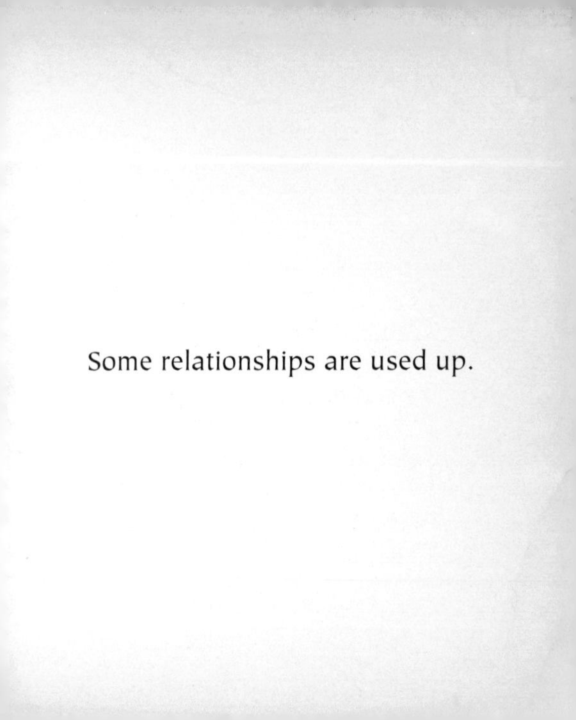

Some relationships are used up.

'I don't know if I love you.'

'I need some time out.'

'I just want some space.'

'I need to sort myself out.'

'I don't know what I want.'

Translation . . .

. . . 'You are on trial,' *or*

'I have another lover,' *or*

'I want another lover.'

There's no kind way of leaving
someone, only a clean way.

No fault divorce?

Usually it's both fault,

but not necessarily in equal parts.

One of us made a choice that led

to us breaking up . . .